To My Companion

To My Companion
within the room within the room

―――――――

Sarah H. Paulson

●
The 3 Lights Press
(2021)

front (detail) and back cover art:
Laura C. Stelmok, *Genesis 2: To bear Her opening, 3 knees*, 2020

In 2018, Laura C. Stelmok invited me to join her in an annual winter residency in Whitefield, Maine.

The poems in this small book are the beginning of an ongoing dialogue of love and serve as a living document of our time together.

Through the heart of my Teacher.

So sacred is this space, in the cave of the heart,
given like a valentine across god's sea
to two friends who are remembering how to hear
through the emptiness of the ear.

To my companion –

The companion in my heart gives to thee a pen with which to write the names of god as they come through the stories of those gathered. I cannot say who I am, nor can you say who you are, but what we know is that we return to our deaths with light in our hearts as a direct result of this gathering. My companion is a tree, a companion of the oldest kind, and the love between us will never, ever, take us from the path. The oneness that she is is fully accessible, unadulterated.

The song in me cries to the song in you. Will you sing with me, please? Will you lay your weapons down so the fire may burn pure again? I don't care about your faults, your mistakes, your madness. It is you who I love, the ancient song that cries to all through one. Will you take your hand as I take mine and walk through the valley of fear? Will you remember my name as I give yours back to you, as I walk backwards into you?

So many pleas have taken us before, but the love that you have shown, have revealed, has destroyed the separation to which I have clung. I will go with you, now and forever, into the wild and back again and again and again. How our hearts have never known the agony at the heart of the world. Oh, but they do. They do. They do.

A pen, the light. The paper, a tree. I give myself to thee and you to me. Together we are marked. You put your hand upon my head; I look up. I ask, "Who has forgotten this old ancient chain to which we were born? Have they forgotten your face?" And you look at me, show your face and cry a song I had long forgotten. I thank you.

> Your companion through eternity.
> [Song of Genesis retreat, 2018]

1.

I have flooded,
waiting for that one to whom I wrote my existence.
Lifetimes of lost love have endured
for independence and reliance to kiss
so your fidelity and betrayal could be received.

How envious I had become when you strayed from me,
fell down and got up without a glance when I lent my eyes,
acknowledged my presence but chose to run.
You have left me for yourself,
your glowing image of life upon us,
your dream of rapture.
And here I have cried at empty wells
for more years than I can remember,
thirsty for your secretions, the love that I adored.
I can barely recall your fragrance,
the feeling of your breath within my chest.
I can barely recall what it's like to recognize a hand of
salvation.

And then I arrived at this streetlamp, broken, torn,
cynical through all of my being.

My heart was given to those who pray,
or those who've forgotten how to pray,
or those who beg to pray or to be prayed for.

"What is prayer?!" she yells, drowning in her own tears.
Here, we are the connections between our lives of anguish,
not to save or fight or even to respond, but to fall together,
to descend into the dark that beckons to the lost one,
the silent one, the insidious one, in all.

She speaks silently from the depths of her own disease,
unwilling to take a breath until we show our insides,
bare our bellies to the stench that we've attributed to her.

Will you outstretch your arm to her,
when she is the face you have denied?
Will you give her your crumpled poem, saved in your coat
pocket, meant to remind you of the love you once had?
Will you endure her remarks or her silence?
Will you receive how she marks you with her gaze?
Will you show the passion she arouses in you,
in spite of your disgust?
Will you give your pen to her to reshape your previous
words?

If your answer is "no,"
you've come to the wrong place.

If your answer is "no,"
you've chosen your journey on your own.
If your answer is "no,"
you've left your homes and families in vain.
If your answer is "no," have you *really* chosen to be lost?

If your answer is "yes,"
we do not know what the future holds,
what she will give and what she will take.
And we will not know, until the story is told,
how your hand will be marked and in what state you will return.

And if your answer continues to be "yes,"
your terror will find you by speaking with her,
and surprise there will be in such company.

And even so, inside her chambers of darkness,
this company of friends will remain,
uncherished by the external world
but precious to her relatives.
She unites them and is the instrument of them,
as they sing her into movement,
determining how she will obey.

We are her children,
following in the footsteps of her secret dance,

choosing freedom through bondage, her actions noted.
We are her daughters, oh lovers of the sun.

How we will be forgotten is a gift of such design,
and how we will remember is her service,
implanted in our bodies.
We covet her no longer, imprisoned by her beauty;
our ugliness is washed and swept up by those who hate her.

She is the sparrow that speaks lies
to those who don't believe in truth,
delivering to them their own defenses.
She is the one who sings to the unborn children
requiring song to be sung into existence.
She is the one who takes your own dilution
and drowns you in your own fears,
until your power and your weakness
are the only breaths you take.
She reaches your beginning,
only to steal your human heart.

She is that ancient.

2.

I came to see you yesterday but you denied my presence.
You left me without a body
and you wandered from home to home —
you knew nothing of your position to that home.
You left home to find nothing except that eternal home.

Fires were put out by your deception.
Colors mixed and your palette became murky.
Language, the sentient being passed from mouth to mouth,
heart to heart, soul to soul, collided with buildings
and became part of the material world.
The unseen beings, in some ways, did the same.
We learn to cover our mistakes by adapting.

If we were to die of shame and unworthiness,
would it be the end?
Who determines the end of suffering?
When does suffering become the recognizable mark?

The medium is limited when the paper refuses ink.

A bird flew through my window,
delivering this message:
> *The birds of this time contain maps that can assist us.*

Will you listen to me now? Will you hear me
when I demonstrate that union will deliver us?

Or will you cage the bird, wisdom and all,
asking it to adapt its wisdom to yours,
asking it to repeat your words,
erasing its language like an imagination trained by an intruder?

3.

Life begins like a maturing fire,
looked after by the officiants of ancient rites,
or today, by those who pray for locations
(physical and immaterial) on this changing land.

If presence has been granted, delivered me to now,
and my pores and body hair,
my full self as earth within the Earth —
all 360 degrees of me —
why couldn't the whole of my lifetimes live in this room?
No beginning and no end,
contained in one room inside these streams of color,
governed by Time but timeless within.

"Drink, my friend," the sheikh said to her student,
after countless lifetimes. "Drink; for the water of eternity
will quench the thirst of a thousand lives."
No truer tale of oneness could there be.

The entrance is within you and of you.
Be one, as the entrance. Together.

Do not drop paper or pen or story, or self,
to choose this or that.
Stay of the ground, of the earth, inside the sun,
like dusk living in the animals —
not the animals responding to dusk.

You cannot make a performance of this;
you can only be in the beauty of your birth.

Leave her now,
that girl who attributes right or wrong,
good or bad, success or failure.

Lay down your history and be recited.
So great is this pleasure of yours:
To be given back into language like fur is given to bear.

Now there is nothing to remove.

4.

For you, in unfinished form,
I give myself.
In my despair,
my broken bones,
my apathy and excitation.

My arrogance, my devotion,
my undeveloped imagination.

Brown and Gold, my dear,
for you from me, at your request.

Brown for your eyes,
the soil, the darkness of your caverns.
My confusion and adoration.

The beauty of brown,
its multitude of terrain.
Its silence,
its wetness,
its arid climate.

Your brown is the most magnificent.
Majesty in her purest form.

The color that *is* color,
forgotten to the unnaked eye.

You gift me with your history:
past and future.

The soil for the rooting.

The basis of devotion to her songs,
her voice, a humble beginning.

Take me to her, please;
settle me down inside her pastures.
Erase me from this culture.

Brown,
dried blood,
dead leaves,
the sacred coffin.

I leave my soil to become you, your limbs,
and you return me back to my time, over and over;
I will not stray.

And I offend you with my sharp speech.
You deliver the words "Brown and Gold"
like the only perfume left in all the world.
Delivered to my unkempt tongue
like rain dissolving poison.

How does one receive the gift of color
though word via heart
at the center of a miracle?

Hidden.
How little there is of this direct line.

And still, "Brown and Gold,"
spoken like a blade,
received *us* with caution and care,
and gave us to this room.

She's come before in her own colors,
the child who knows her name
before her birth.

Brown like your eyes,
the value of earth,
the premonition of the future,
and the graves of our fathers and mothers.

And to you, gold.
I give to thee your gold,
your ring of wonder,
a reflection polished pure,
the gate to that unknown brown.
I give you my hand in marriage,
merging your ingredients,
your love of this world.
I give to you the understanding that dominates nothing
except that which saveth her heavy hand.

All with love,
the kiss of death before Death.

We wish for excuses,
and we share meals,
break bread not speaking of this moment,
not listening for this moment.

I cannot tell you how many times
I have mistakenly taken her colors,
remembering them through her,
not acknowledging her presence,
her insistence upon the complete story.

Even in her fractured state she stands for justice.

A leaf fell from me to you.
I caught it as a wisp from another world.
I opened it, shocked by the declaration
that your love is close,
is rapturous,
is my command to stay.

5.

When did I forget your name?
When did I forget your hands?
(These are the secret questions I whisper beneath my
covers.)

How long has it been since I've tasted your lips?
I've cried so many tears that I remain dry,
my waters deserted.
How have you remained faithful
when I've forgotten your name?
Have you remained faithful?

Have you believed the path a journey,
or have you taken to your bed?

Do you hear me when I recite empty poetry
or watch me when I try to recall the shape of dance?
Do you mock me when I draw mountainscapes,
mastery long forgotten?
Do you judge me when I approach the Master Point,
uncertain of my worthiness?

Do you experience boredom when I try to meditate?
Do you see my flaws when I enter relationship?
Do you know my fire that burns eternally?
Will you stand for my madness, even in my shadow?

I don't know where you've gone or
who you've chosen to companion.
I don't remember if I'm to speak to you or
if you're to speak to me.

I've forgotten manners, my mind, and my needs.
I know not even trust.

Will you find me?
Sick and mortal and of the eternal?
Will you sign for me, as I signed for you when I arrived,
pure and confused, destined for such departure?

Will you show me your nature?
I've forgotten how to invite you.
Will you unwed me and marry me?
I've forgotten the bond that birthed me.

Will you remind me, recite me, devour me, and tame me?
Will you live inside me?
Will you destroy me?

6.

There's nothing real.
No sound, no movement,
no sincere gesture or reliable account.
The sources say somewhere that we've reached eternity
where time collides with space in a commingling that
neither exists nor ceases to exist.

I have no idea where I come from,
nor where I'm going nor even where I am.
I remember one day, not long ago,
being given to the present,
trained to breathe and sleep there;
but *present* to me means nothing now.
Is there a letter to be written?
Or a word to be received?
Or a sound to be uttered or responded to?

The teacher pours water upon me in my bed
in the middle of the night!
More water, *please*.

But no, I don't dwell here; I don't dwell anywhere.
I have no image inside me, no word, no direction, no desire.
No future, no past, no knowledge.

I watch my hand write,
and I know nothing of where it has been.
I see red ink, and I can't remember color.
I care not for life or things or people or thoughts.
I forgot my niceties at the door.
I can't read poetry or advice or human subtlety.
I live nowhere, inside you,
like a dream unable to surface,
dormant but living.
Expressions cannot capture me;
I am incapturable.

If life could pay me, I wouldn't know money.
If children could sing to me, I've never had ears.
I am underneath all that you do, all that you speak,
all that you see, all that you seek.
I am nowhere.
You are somewhere; I don't know where.

We feel around in the dark not recognizing texture,
or shape, or form, or time.
Has time forgotten us, like a blanket abandoned by summer?
Has our eye contact swallowed us whole,
giving us to the masses without an objection,

devoured by the wild dogs of our minds?
Has earth cracked open revealing her fire?
Have we witnessed it?
Have we become it like a vulture eating a fresh carcass?

Have you tasted anything of my body?
I don't remember smell.
I used to grapple with my shape;
now I have none to give or steal or alter or hide.

I left you triumphantly like a bird in the night,
all my plumes given to the darkness,
stealing your knowledge and granting your wish.
I could return you, but your silence becomes you.

You cannot hope or dream or write or speak.
Such is the mystery of time beyond the present.
You shook hands with him once, the Master of cycles.
Not long ago, you shook hands as friends.
And now, either he has forgotten you,
or he has abolished you,
lending a hand in mortal forgetfulness.
He is loyal to you as you enter him, past him,
time beyond Time.

They speak of riches and glory and intoxicating love,
but here, no.

You'll drown like a single sorrow, no memory,
no guidance, no word to call home.
No end and no beginning.

We face one another in absence of form
and speak without moving, unbridled by nothingness.

The empty cavern, it waits.
It is situated in the center.
Souls enter and leave, and enter and leave
like carrier pigeons without a home.

You sacrifice your tongue, your body, your unknown facts.
Slowly you return deeper and deeper,
transcending nothing and no one,
not even your self.
The fires are water, her insides of mirth.
You are stepped upon in transparency, pain long gone.

"The angels are jealous of us," once an echo in the wind.
Here, jealousy disperses;
the borders between realms cease.

"Where are you, my faithful daughter?"
I cannot hear it in myself.
I am forbidden to ask or answer.
And days upon days may be a thousand years in an evening.

The explanations and records have lost their meaning.

7.

A poem left its scent on my fingertip and I obeyed.
I opened the land within myself
to elaborate on the meaning of word,
and I came upon an island within my chest.
It had been covered, this ancient and alive body of land.
It recognized me when I parted myself to see it.
The tides were awake; they knew my face.
I climbed upon her closest rock
and discovered that she knew my weight.
I found my footing and proceeded to climb,
higher and higher.
This island was of the north.
I needed only to follow the land.

After hours of exploration, I came upon a book,
the words which won't reveal themselves to me now.
I reached in my pocket and discovered a pen.
Asking for direction, I retraced the pen's movements.
I learned that language arrives through dance,
inseparable as mediums (dance and language).
My memory was wiped clean,
and my past no longer pulled me.

I put the pen down on the book
thinking someone else might need it to write,
but the pen got up and inserted itself back into my pocket.
The book opened itself to this page and folded down
its own corner.
Here and onward were empty,
but across the top of this page read:

> *Your contribution will be overshadowed by fate.*
> *Begin here now.*

There are nights when the poems come
and nights when they lay dry,
disinterested in the beauty they might prepare.
It is the seeker's job to follow the words as they arrive,
not determine their arrival.

The ancient texts were written like rainwater
being collected by the thirsty.
There would be days that called for a hundred buckets
and weeks that would call for none.
If the bead of dew happened upon you,
you would join in communion,
holy worship through companionship and word,
silent for most of the working hours.
Thirsty you would come and thirstier you would leave,
your body wanting something more than it has known.

The subtlety of direct correspondence is that it must pass
through your heart and change you in the process.
You are not saying the words,
but you are receiving them like landmarks in time.
The wind passes through the tree branches,
sometimes rustling the leaves,
and sometimes leaving the branches bare,
and sometimes whispering a song unlikely to occur at any
other time.

If I give you a secret, will you promise not to discard it?
Yes.

You are in anticipation of the drowning man's words.
Remain marked.
He will need a voice when the time comes,
when the longing is so great.
Until then, remain in practice;
the book will prepare you.
Listen as you do, even when listening has reached its end.

You've been captured by the ego's demise,
the very request you made last night.
The nature of your muse is to ask,
and typically, you are taken seriously.

Settle down.   Feel the words as they come.

Don't jump ahead or behind or even underneath.
The practice in presence, however momentary,
trains you in this relationship between pen and ink,
between inbreath and outbreath.

Change your understanding of what focus is.
The life of the artist is spent in prayer,
in speech and in silence, in production and dormancy.

Every door has another door.
Every word another word within.
You will find desolation there,
and heartache, and forgetfulness.
You will find sorrow and unexplainable overwhelm.

You will seek cover,
but once you enter you best not turn back,
if you are welcomed in.
If you leave too soon you risk stealing the word,
not by intention but because words are revealed,
and you are welcomed into deeper states or different states.
In these states, you are changed,
altered to be the language that was given to you.
If you depart too early, you do not respect the realms
and you are unchanged in the rightful way.

Free will is different in Hurqalya.
Free will is different in the Blue Room.
Free will is your greatest obstacle when freedom leads.
The silent sighs of the sages who have come before us
tell us this truth.

Do not lose your pen as you lose your self.
Holy, holy is this failure.

8.

Dear Ezekiel,

I am left without direction, without strength of mind.
I am allergic to my sins.
I see the drawings burning —
the idols and symbols within ourselves.
Who is saving our dying people
when our insides are turning to ash?
Is there more space for new symbols,
new language, and birth?
Are we hollowed for eternity,
or is one space enough for the whole?

I have no idea who you are,
but I write to you from this time,
this room in the heart of the one who knows
the heart of the world.

I've been baking bread,
too indignant to share it.
What will come of those symbols
when the shadows come between us?

I have learned that the hand is inside a holier hand,
the hand given, and given again.
If consciousness doesn't come as action is passed forward,
the bread will rot, digested by no one.
If we were to give our names to our word,
the promise of our lives would be given to the children.
Without the living signature, the burning has no end.

But birth we must do first;
the rhythm and respect of being birthed must lead.
I had forgotten this until now.
Your sacred ones came through the cracks,
arriving carrying candles like nights that found their souls.

There is a subtle humming that I hear from far away.
Perhaps your pain was questioned like your brothers
who held you free.

Your gravesite lives inside of me,
companioned within this friendship from which I write.
Stories live here, fires, stonings, mass persecution,
extinction of species, emergence of culture, desecration
of consciousness, injured lives, vows of silence, betrayals,
eternal love, forgiveness, trespasses, bombs and more
bombs, stolen traditions, secret traditions, lights hidden in
the earth.

If you've been forgotten, we have too.
I've lost the ribbon that bound me to my self,
and I won't escape, won't leave my drowning post.

The light, it still comes through the circle of infinity,
a keyhole left open for those whose shape is gifted to a time.

I am not your sister, or your brother, or mother or father.
I wish for all our faces to become true.
I sacrificed my blood this morning
and discovered there is another sun inside this earth.
It was sent as you were sent, I think,
like heaven's only wish.
Only you were a person and it a sun,
and within both, the sun of suns that unites us all.

We do not know how to transcribe wailing or
how to give it back to the trees.
Our voices are untrained, and volume only incites chaos.
Where do we turn except to One when hope, or fear,
or anger, or comfort, or addiction have nothing to do with
knowledge, and knowledge in us is only in presence?

I know not who you are,
but I heard your name within my heart.

9.

If I left a note on the table with your name on it,
would you read it and take it to heart?
Would you know that it came from my heart
if it was addressed to you?

Or would you discard it without reading,
expecting that the words would come to you
in some other way?

You would not do the latter.
I *hope* you would not do the latter.
You would give yourself to the script that was written to you
by you, and you would, god-willing,
reply accordingly. You would.
Would you?

Repentance.
You are faced with the words, to yourself,
from yourself, or another, and you give yourself
to the history of that relationship:
Past, present or future.
(Or all three in one.)

To arrive here, you must look toward
the old one who sits before you.
For repentance to awaken,
you must be led by the seed within her.
A seed is within this wisdom;
what will come is held by the dying.
In this relationship, past and future merge:
Eternity.

Repentance *is* every breath.
Repentance *can be lived* in every breath.
Teacher within teacher within teacher within teacher.
Student within student within student within teacher.
Within the two together.
The blooming is in the darkness,
visible only to those willing to be blinded by beauty,
or life for the season.

By awe we are positioned.
Such is this Residency.
Such is the dream that calls one back
when she's lost her way.
Such is the love between lovers that can destroy,
break one to weakness and point one's crown
towards the ground.

To land at the feet of this teacher:

Is it repentance?
Is it submission?
Is it awe or beauty or wonder?
Is it the service to life herself?
Is it the word made true?
Is it the requirement for love?
Is it the breath of god reducing one to her essence?
Is it here, now, that we can grasp
the multitude of dimensions,
the impartial call in every word or footprint on the path?
(Yes.)

Your devotion will carry you
only so far as you know devotion.
Until devotion can open, within, again and again,
the meaning of words can only go so far as they are called.
So through a doorway,
like that day with the friend in the desert land,
we witness the preparation of the entrants.

Repentance is planted, day by day, second by second.
We read this letter and step with care,
as if each atom, each particle knows its place,
and has been found.
Knowing that we are found, lost and deprived of ourselves.
Knowing that we are carried by dust of the wildest kind —
intelligent and sensory.

The sacredness of a moment is lost day after day.
(We lost that friend in the desert,
that one whose eyes saw salvation.)
The sacredness of a life is lost, person after person.

I ask that you step toward what is waiting,
not as a triumphant gift to the world, but as a breath,
delivered and inhaled by this room for which you long.

The isolation of failing to fulfill
this simple warning will make you ineffectual,
and the greatest kind of human fear will prevail.

Take this letter to heart and let down the guard of pride,
in the name of your given name written in your own letter.

10.

Inside the earth is a valley that has no end.
The end of that valley marks an entrance
void of landmarks in our world.
Without an ancestral line of spirit,
the entrance cannot be approached.
It cannot be recognized.

If the world contained another world,
that is how we would speak of what is behind that door.
When one is led through,
recognized as one who must tread upon this wooden
floor of open stories and unexplained masterpieces,
one becomes a part of this tapestry,
a ray of sun inside a sunlit room,
hidden by darkness, located through light.

Within us is an omnipotent bondservant,
free with the power of resolution
to become an aspect of ourselves.
We are stamped early,
perhaps even before arrival,

as the almighty's own being.

This door holds the contract of the agreement within.
It is readable only by candlelight,
lit with the heart of memory.
By remembering, we may read it.
Upon reading, we are marked, again.

To weep is the mandate in this moment,
in the presence of this early promise.
Tears of unknowing, of fear, of reprise,
and of knowledge never granted
water this seed (covered but not fully forgotten).
So this seed may be read as light through illumination.
When light meets light,
the senses are transformed.

Ecstasy is known privately
by she who is devoted to word.
How one must hold her tongue!
Those that are called toward color or fabric
or texture or dance wait to be infused
with this divine instruction.

Like a dragonfly upon the edge of a canoe,
it takes balance to live on that line
between the vast and the finite.

Take care not to abandon true home
in this double-edged location
where culture's language is learned and spoken.
The pull to drown is strong,
and the pull to fly, take off, abandon the mystery of this
narrow edge can overpower even the deepest of ascetics.

We must bow before the ones who have come before us,
though we can never see their journeys.
Their failings teach us to pray for the freedom of bondage,
not neglect the price paid for their neglect.

When the dragonfly departs,
these words disappear.

11.

If I had cried a thousand tears last night,
my eyes would be drowned in your image.
I cannot say I know my worth
or the price I'm willing to pay to see you again,
but in my heart, I am built to last,
to endure the censorship placed upon my devotion
and deliverance to you.

I've wept so many times on the inside,
not knowing the purpose of outward tears.
I've asked the world of my organs to hold this growing flood.
Is it in their nature to keep my secret?
Or is it my ego's response to the distaste of my people?
Is it fear that the tears will be stolen and turned against me,
separating us from eternal longing?
Or is it me, separation's prisoner,
commanding you to remain locked in solitude,
prohibiting you from entering the world within?

Am I that jealous?
Is my selfishness this true?

Will I die a firm believer that our love cannot be publicked?
Will you give me a hint, to understand this binding?
…this confusion?
…this secret of secrets?

If I turned inside out and the world could see
the ocean of my madness, would you still be inside me?
I keep my secrets hidden, and still I overflow,
like a lake after years of constant rain.

We cannot see my outline;
I've been drunk by my waters.
I've been sacrificed to the oxen who drink,
who bow their heads as they take a sip of me.
I've left nothing dry, I am so old.
I needn't hunt or search or find or show.

You have taken me,
drenched me in myself with your glory.

12.

When the sky in myself is eclipsed by such sadness,
I cannot breathe.
If breath is the master, how does one follow in this state?
If I am to be aware of my breath,
how do I know if I exist without this action,
without this prayer?
If I am to forget prayer, will I be forgotten?
Will I have sacrificed my life in vain?
Will my sacrifice be thievery?
Will I be guilty of betrayal?

If the sacrifice is *not* in vain,
what does the breath beyond the breath feel like?
What does the breath within the breath breathe?
But I cannot ask these questions
if I take sadness under my coat,
a dark friend cocooning me,
making forgetfulness part of my excuse.

How does one love as an ex-lover?
How does one speak as an ex-lover?

How does one return to the lover
like a solemn prayer soaked in laughter
when joy is not the window I look through?

Help this poor soul be the kind of broken lover
unforgotten by her own sacrament.

If this is my only request,
how does one receive rain during drought?
How does one become the darkness beneath your armpit,
cloaked by the breath of every pore,
saturated by every droplet of sweat,
cradled by the human inside the holiness of a vehicle
given by the heavens of creation?

If our questions could come, undisclosed to judging ears,
holy fear could be returned to voice
and longing returned to longed for.

13.

Follow me past your certainty,
back before texts were written to be read or spoken.
Follow me back before language was in the hands of men,
meant to obliterate and separate.
Follow me before the word was given to you.
Rewind your mind before speech.
Say the first word like it is the only word,
containing all the words,
forever.

She is that movement —
that severance from a life of separation.
She comes to you as you come to her,
and together that substance of compenetration
is what seeds light. That is the feminine way.

Two women,
face to face, body to body,
turning toward the entrance in themselves,
from the message that can speak to and
instruct those very women.

We are made of flesh and blood
so that we may house the gates
that open to her body, her soul.

You come from very far away
to assist her body in reopening in you.
We are sent far, some of us,
to become the garden that can be tended.
So dare not to abandon her vines,
each one with a whisper.

But do not get distracted;
she tests each one of us singly,
building our capacity to receive her.
The heartache that she is
is only a veil meant to ask us to account for
the heartache in ourselves.
She cannot be expected to play a role
when the performance enters the eye of Her.
She is the performance —
one skin, one body, one scent.

She trains us to see her,
and if allowed, endured, and born,
she becomes —

14.
The Sage and the Ear,
A Warning

For many years, the texts were returned in a lawful way to the sages, but there came a time when this did not please the public. Everyone wanted the texts that came through the cracks. With their wanting, the people forgot their own value and sought to find it outside of themselves.

So the sages remained quiet and humble about their knowledge. They read letters between one another by writing in this very way. They could hear the listening and the questions between the gates within this inner network.

The ill-will that eventually found its way through the cracks altered the purity of the signals sent between the sages. Though they could still hear through the dissonance, the sages had to work hard to keep their doorways clean, for they never knew who might arrive or what message might be sent.

At the foot of the entrance to every gate was an ear that was kept empty, day and night. Its emptiness was fundamental for the words of the day, or the time, or even many future years, to be received. Sometimes the words would come like a downpour, never stopping except by the force of seasonal change. At other times, the winds swept across vast plains, and the ear remained open, clear, clean, never anticipating the moment when word would be sent again.

One day, the sage walked through the gate and into the ear in order to hear what might be coming. The emptiness of the ear was filled with the sage's presence. The ear lost its place and became flooded with debris. The position of the sage to the ear was no longer the promised one, so the balance was thrown off and the ear forgot how to hear.

The sage had stretched her own ears in order to call the message forth, and the relationship to time between all the gates became confused. The natural balance began to deplete, and the sages were no longer protected. Some remained, but it became much more difficult for them, and the value of the word decreased as it was pulled into the world for buying and selling.

15.

I feel how I belong to paper, the earth,
and receive from heaven, the pen,
as a tree soaks water from above and below.
We all are imprints from the great master;
when duty cannot be fulfilled,
great sadness fills our heart.

For us, the heart is washed like an infant
received by the world for the first time.
We are washed like the dying, on their way out,
the exit of wonder and mystery.
To return to one we are tuned in the cycles
given to this planet.

Gravity is a force that holds us to such magnificent rotation.
And we find this force in ourselves, as well,
like beings returned to a place that needs our presence,
as much as we need the place.

When my face was turned toward this world,
I saw nothing but destruction and desecration.
And then, my face was turned away

and I couldn't be separate —
I was one, inside of one
at the position of zero inside of myself.

And then, I was turned back towards this world
and destruction was no longer.
I could see beauty in every living thing,
and my young mind wondered whose eyes
I had worn in that previous glance.
It would have become a promise to stay turned away,
but I couldn't find the solution to my madness
by separating myself through non-separation.
So I returned, out of need and requirement.

I have tasted both worlds.
They today still clash within, but further in,
they form a partnership where, indeed, dead fish come alive
and the inner and outer intermingle like the bird of life
and the bird of death embracing during flight.
Inhale and exhale.

She knows no one like you.
And you know no one like her.
This living breathing well of earth
upon which we have been placed
penetrates the darkness within my mind
and leads me to the cave where I was born.

Today.
Of all days, today.

Birth is in the moment,
and death is in our eyes like an endangered lion
kept alive on the inside by the promise of that other world.
He waits for you like the lioness births her cubs.

In this seat, you will see many come and many go,
like robbers returning to their homes
after gathering the stolen goods.
It is not your business to judge, only to stay.

Stay in your seat.

Weep only tears that connect you to the soil.
Sever nothing that holds this seat to you and you to it.
Be careful in your reflections not to wander too far
when the map is one-pointed.

Pen to page. Head in heaven, feet in earth.
Position of prayer. The arabesque of the divine.

A double-meaning inside of life
meant to keep you hunting for the hint,
hunted by the master, sacrificed to yourself
in a time where good and evil have battles ahead.

Remain distinct but not advertised.
Stretch with your life. Do not stretch your life —
it is not yours to keep.

16.

If there were a poem to be written,
from where would it come?
If my heart had the words, how would it deliver?
If my teacher were inside me and I inside my teacher,
would my words be true?
If she found me, so long ago,
when despair covered my orifices,
I must know that the bond is only ever with the beloved.
I would know, I do know, that this light is singular;
this light is needed.

This light is my home.
This light is watched over,
tended in its life like a student
of an old and experienced teacher,
holding the space for life to come.
This path leads nowhere.

I can hear the laughter even through my own crimes,
my apathy, my unapologetic dedication to where I've been.
I can hear the laughter, most especially,
in those early years of torture.

I never knew I would land here,
and yet the protections asked me to stay close.
And so I did.

If I could forget one thing,
it would be how I closed my eyes to the world.
But if I don't remember, I will not stay awake
to how we've forced the world into devastation.

So would I forget? No.

I fear I remember too much and not enough.
I forgot myself for many years, so I created myself daily.
I reminded myself of my body.
And I protected that poet, or that light,
with all of my power.
I tricked those who thought they knew me,
and I asked that voice inside to stay quiet but close,
so I would not forget the promise.
And I was asked to share my secret dozens of times,
and I declined.

To live for a task, one must be trained in all seasons of life —
in youth, in development, in depression, and in ecstasy.
We know the worlds include us if we dare to speak
to and through them.
We must remain present, here at the end.

We must remain present for the words to open
into a whole country (or world of origin),
to be given back to the heart between us.

The word or substance is green, like the first taste,
and the practice is black.
That is the performance.
(Now is too early to speak.)

The light between you is given into the soul of Friendship,
like milk given to the infant.
The mouths have been empty, open, gaping.
They must be given something to say.
They must be cared for.
It is not your job to care for them,
but you must know when you have been fed.
And you have.

You have something to say, to return.
To swallow love allows the secret of the heart
to be awakened in honor of the dying wish,
the last question, inside the soul.
Like the firefly lighting a particular moment of the night,
this meeting does this.
The meeting of love with the earth.
The meeting of light *without* with the light *within*.
The penetration of the hand of the master,
through time, and into the heart of the student,

lighting the way by feel and memory.
So secret is the guiding.
So guided is the guiding.
One cannot be present without the other:

I left for you a promise on a table inside your deepest longing. You will read it when there is nothing else left, and you will remember that this has been waiting all along. And your adab must help you to be guided as to how to approach this table. What hand receives and what hand gives? What date to speak and what date to cease?

My years are infinite. Yours are finite. I am, inside of you, and your life given to me. I have seen a thousand yous and you belong to only one of me. I watch for you day and night; I always have. And you've spoken to me — a channel long forgotten. If I stay with you, you will stay with me. I will teach you the miracle of binding so that you may give me to my own teaching. You know the key is in your heart, turned by the teacher or me. Inside that keyhole is a place, a darkness with no end, where she, the teacher, and I, the soul, meet, and eternity dies inside such fire of love. This is the secret to the making of a servant. Unobstructed, unintruded. Free.

17.

To the world I love:

Your messages have not been received by your children.
We have left a trail of rubbish upon your lands,
like idiots thinking you, world, would save us when we
refused to do it ourselves.

I find comfort in how you speak to us today.
Your subtle breath coupled with nature's revenge call out,
cry out to the agony in each of us.

Can I deny my current connection to you? No!
This time is killing us,
and we've warped even our purest of warriors.
I do know that love still exists.
I do know that there are some that still know this.
Know that I know this. *Please.*

We behave silently,
completely giving ourselves over and over again
to the way time turns us.

You turn too, not a flavor, but a song.
Is there a song of resurrection?
Or is there only the death song?

I call to no one in my sleep,
and when faced with the woman
who was wearing another face,
I went through her eyes, entering terror,
both of us shaking inside the technology
of what we call music.
And I called out, "Laura!"

I am absent of my body and mind here,
and I wonder how you cope.
You cannot be empty of body;
you were made of terrain and spirit and fire and water,
and you hold flesh and blood,
and you feel and are fueled by breath,
the rain of creation.

How can I love with you?
How can I speak alongside of you?
How can I face the past —
my wrongdoings and sacrifices made to false gods?
How can I return the gift of life I was given as this human
that I am to your ever-present receptivity?
How can my anger interact with the anger of those who

throw stones at your feminine passion?
How can the youth in me speak to the old in me so language
may speak to you as you perish?

I ask you, my trusted friend,
as a friend unworthy of your trust.
I wish the world, *for you*,
would hear herself burning with you.
I wish we could follow that our deaths live *with* your death.
But we are a literal culture.
We take *tests* out of context.
We forget and deny the sacred hint.
We speak only in verbal language and act with deception.

We are a futile state.

No words have reached you in me — not yet.
And still I ask: How can this be turned?
How can I be turned to watch your dying face,
so you can see your beauty?
How can I speak directly to you
through the living of my remaining years?
Who will die first?
I believe we are dying together.
Are we?
Will you be sent somewhere else, you old being?
Will we be together?

So ancient are your mountains;
so dangerous are your divisions.
So full of wisdom are your waters;
so poisonous are your seas.
If I could count on my hand how many times
we have left you, I would have no more hands —
I never through eternity would have had hands.
But I do have hands.
They have been lent to me to stand upon you
and to reach upward toward the heavens,
with your blessing.

3 Lights: Heaven. Human. Earth.

When the lights go out,
where will the light of heaven and the light of earth go?
Where will they go on the inside?
Where will they go on the outside?
Where will they go within me?
Where will they go within you?
Will they perish with us?
Or will they conjoin with our spirits?
Will there be only one?
Or will there be a million worlds,
separating us through multiplicity?

I call upon the water within

that knows soil cannot be divided,
that water cannot be owned.

It is not paradise we are stepping toward.
It is the response to our decay.
The death song.
Her song of Resurrection.

Will the intention of heaven
have the power to penetrate earth?
Will the earth that is you and the earth within me
be prepared to receive the master gardener's prayer of song?
That master gardener is not from this world.
We are the soil, and we need water.

Please, we must not harden, must not become too ancient
or historical before we can be used.
Please, we must not be caught in the past
before our time comes.
We must befriend time here and now.

I will learn to live this change.
Will you? You need not answer.
My lifetime has tread upon your transitions.
I have been breathed by you in all weather.
Will we be ignited into conversation?
I will carry this question for you, for us, for life to come.

I hear the whisper of humanity's voice,
resurrected by creation.

Let this witness be given the name *miracle*,
as they say in duality.

Let the secret mystery approach us. Your soul and mine.
Let us weep for warmth. Let this story live, just for one day.

When the lost secrets of a lifetime are left for another, continents in the soul converge and a blooming occurs. If the standard practice were to pick that flower, the life of the soul would be limited; so the teacher blooms alongside that flower, blocking wind at times and whispering the presence of the sun at others.

SARAH H. PAULSON is an artist, writer, and acupuncturist. She believes that performance, in its sacred form, is connected to the mystery of what it is to be human. She lives with her husband in Putney, Vermont.

www.sarahhpaulson.com

THE SCHOOL OF 3 LIGHTS, a school for the muse, is housed by The Unseen Hand: Medicine from Antiquity, a non-profit school dedicated to making available the esoteric teachings and practices of an ancient mystical lineage.

www.schoolof3lights.org

www.ingramcontent.com/pod-product-compliance
Lightning Source LLC
Chambersburg PA
CBHW020912080526
44589CB00011B/567